INTO Wild Guyana

BLACKBIRCH PRESS

An imprint of Thomson Gale, a part of The Thomson Corporation

THOMSON
™
GALE

Detroit • New York • San Francisco • San Diego • New Haven, Conn. • Waterville, Maine • London • Munich

LIBRARY OF CONGRESS CATALOGING-IN-PUBLICATION DATA

Into Wild Guyana / John Woodward, book editor.
   p. cm. — (The Jeff Corwin experience)
Based on an episode from a Discovery Channel program hosted by Jeff Corwin.
Summary: Television personality Jeff Corwin takes the reader on an expedition to Guyana to learn about the diverse wildlife found there.
Includes bibliographical references and index.
  ISBN 1-4103-0231-8 (hardback : alk. paper) — ISBN 1-4103-0232-6 (pbk. : alk. paper)
  1. Zoology—Guyana—Juvenile literature. [1. Zoology—Guyana. 2. Guyana—Description and travel. 3. Corwin, Jeff.] I. Woodward, John. II. Corwin, Jeff. III. Series.

Printed in the United States
10 9 8 7 6 5 4 3 2 1

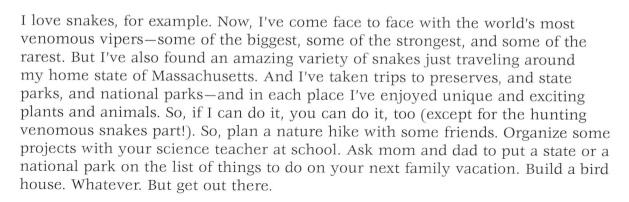

E ver since I was a kid, I dreamed about traveling around the world, visiting exotic places, and seeing all kinds of incredible animals. And now, guess what? That's exactly what I get to do!

Yes, I am incredibly lucky. But, you don't have to have your own television show on Animal Planet to go off and explore the natural world around you. I mean, I travel to Madagascar and the Amazon and all kinds of really cool places—but I don't need to go that far to see amazing wildlife up close. In fact, I can find thousands of incredible critters right here, in my own backyard—or in my neighbor's yard (he does get kind of upset when he finds me crawling around in the bushes, though). The point is, no matter where you are, there's fantastic stuff to see in nature. All you have to do is look.

I love snakes, for example. Now, I've come face to face with the world's most venomous vipers—some of the biggest, some of the strongest, and some of the rarest. But I've also found an amazing variety of snakes just traveling around my home state of Massachusetts. And I've taken trips to preserves, and state parks, and national parks—and in each place I've enjoyed unique and exciting plants and animals. So, if I can do it, you can do it, too (except for the hunting venomous snakes part!). So, plan a nature hike with some friends. Organize some projects with your science teacher at school. Ask mom and dad to put a state or a national park on the list of things to do on your next family vacation. Build a bird house. Whatever. But get out there.

As you read through these pages and look at the photos, you'll probably see how jazzed I get when I come face to face with beautiful animals. That's good. I want you to feel that excitement. And I want you to remember that—even if you don't have your own TV show—you can still experience the awesome beauty of nature almost anywhere you go—any day of the week. I only hope that I can help bring that awesome power and beauty a little closer to you. Enjoy!

Best Wishes!

Jeff

INTO Wild Guyana

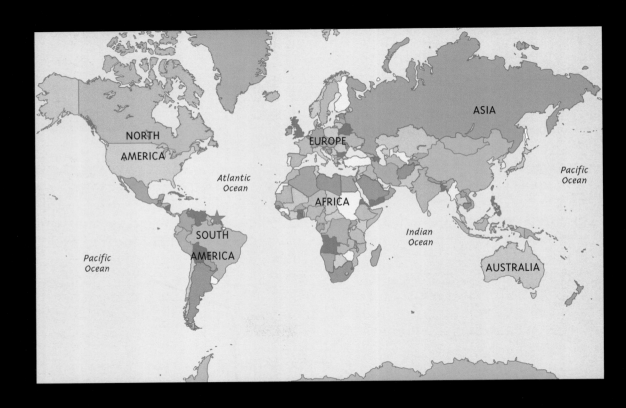

NORTH AMERICA

Atlantic Ocean

SOUTH AMERICA

Pacific Ocean

EUROPE

AFRICA

ASIA

Pacific Ocean

Indian Ocean

AUSTRALIA

Pacific Ocean

It's a small country with some very big creatures. It has one of the tallest waterfalls in the world, some remarkable serpents, and some remarkable people. You may have trouble locating this tiny place on a map, but still I think of it as the land of the giants.

I'm Jeff Corwin.
Welcome to Guyana.

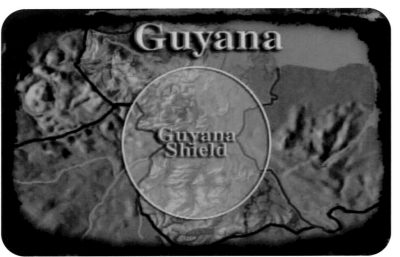

We're on the east coast of South America, bordering the Caribbean Sea. There are lots of countries in South America. In fact, there are lots of tropical countries that contain rain forests. But what makes Guyana very special is that it has the largest tract of undisturbed rain forest in the world. It's huge! It's called the Guyana Shield, and it's a great place for discovery and exploration. My plan is to find some very interesting wildlife.

We're driving along the east coast of South America.

What makes Guyana special is that it has huge tracts of pristine rain forest.

There are some giant species here in Guyana.

I got him!

As countries in South America go, Guyana is pretty small, but it's really big when it comes to wildlife because there are giant species to be found here. In fact, we're going to go look for one right now. I've got Leo and Manny with me. They are masters at finding one very big reptile. Let's go find it.

That turtle is what we're looking for. To get to him, we've got to go in the water. He's moving this way. Look right there! I got him. Look at this turtle. It's huge! This is the giant river turtle. The scientific name is *Podocnemis expansa*. And expansive it is!

Leo is a master turtle catcher. He's going to help pull this creature around so I can show the turtle's face a little more. This type of turtle is the largest freshwater turtle in South America. This one is a female. How do I know? If I turn her up like this and you look at her belly, you can see that it's rounded to make room for eggs. She has flipperlike feet for pushing and digging and swimming. Historically, these turtles were hunted for their flesh and their fat. Their fat was rendered into oil for burning in lamps. What saved these turtles from extinction in the nineteenth century was kerosene. The introduction of kerosene for lamps in this region prevented these animals from being hunted to extinction.

This is one of the last bastions for these animals. They've all but disappeared in other parts of South America. I have seen three wild giant river turtles in my life, and this, by far, is the greatest encounter of them all. Let's return this beauty back to the water.

This is what's wonderful about Guyana. We can explore creatures like this because it's such a pristine habitat. It is so beautiful, and much of it is untouched. It will give us a chance to find animals. Many of them are great in size and for the most part have disappeared in other parts of South America.

Leo here is a master turtle catcher.

There you go. Back into the water.

We're heading south on the Essequibo River ...

Now we're going to head south on the Essequibo and Rupununi rivers. Along the way we'll meet many of the giants that this land is famous for. Our final destination is the savanna that lies at the southern end of this country. Our journey begins on the Essequibo River near a place called Iwokrama.

to a wide open savanna.

I was just walking down this path when suddenly what looks like a stick froze in front of me. It must be as nervous as I am, because its muscles have frozen within its skin. Look at this beautiful parrot snake.

Is that a stick or a snake?

It's one of the many snakes you find living in the rain forest, both up in the canopy and down on the forest floor. It's a beautiful snake. He's got those huge eyes that are perfect for detecting the presence of birds or lizards. This animal is at its best sliding down a branch and hunting creatures like frogs, lizards, or birds. The eyes are set to the front so it can see the twitch of a dulap, the flap of skin under the chin of an anole lizard, or the flicker of a bird's feather.

It's a parrot snake!

These huge eyes can see the slightest movement.

And then, boom! It locks on and swallows its prey. Look at the beautiful, olive-colored camouflage of this snake. We'll let this creature go back to its journey. See how he's puffed up like that? He's filled with air to appear more menacing and terrify the predator that has captured him.

And it just locks onto its prey.

Its olive color is great camouflage.

He's puffing up to scare me.

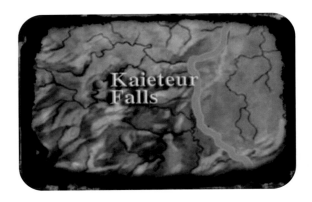

Here's the plane I chartered.

Now I'm going to show you something really big. While at Iwokrama I heard about one of the great natural wonders of the Western Hemisphere. So I charted a plane to take a little detour and see it for myself. It's the famous Kaieteur waterfall, arguably the longest waterfall in the world. It's almost 800 feet tall! It's nearly in the center of Guyana, and its water source is the Essequibo River.

The Kaieteur waterfall may be the longest in the world!

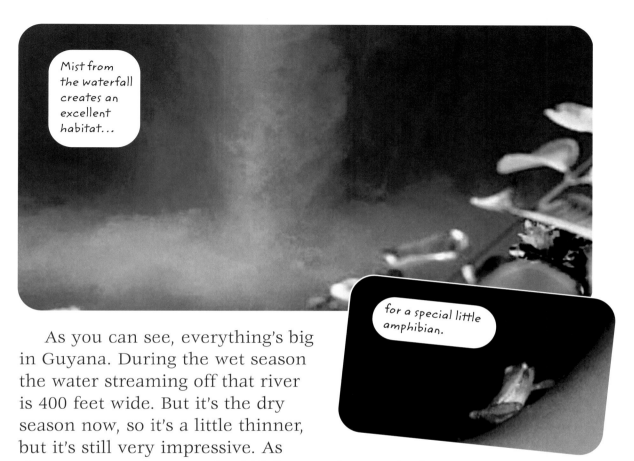

Mist from the waterfall creates an excellent habitat...

for a special little amphibian.

As you can see, everything's big in Guyana. During the wet season the water streaming off that river is 400 feet wide. But it's the dry season now, so it's a little thinner, but it's still very impressive. As that water crashes nearly 800 feet to the earth, it creates a mist that permeates this environment. It creates an excellent habitat for a very special amphibian that is found nowhere else but here. To find it we have to look inside bromeliads.

Check this out. This is a giant tank bromeliad. It's an epiphytic plant, which means it's not absorbing nutrients from the soil. It creates bundles of roots either against rocks or trees. And not only is it surviving, but it's creating a habitat. Remember all that moisture coming off the Kaieteur Falls? Well, it's spreading through these bromeliads and it pools up as water. That source of water becomes a habitat for an amphibian I've always wanted to see. And here it is! I didn't think we were going to find one this quickly. It's this little golden frog.

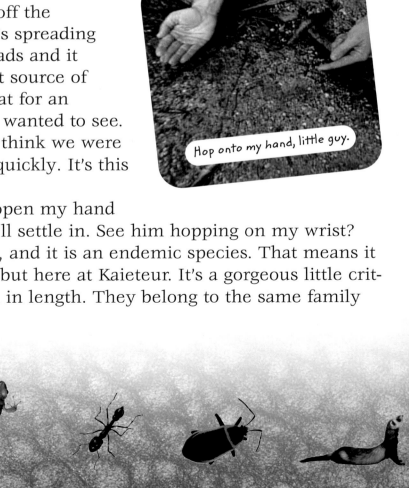

Check out this giant tank bromeliad.

Hop onto my hand, little guy.

I'm going to try to open my hand carefully and see if he'll settle in. See him hopping on my wrist? This is the golden frog, and it is an endemic species. That means it is found nowhere else but here at Kaieteur. It's a gorgeous little critter, only about an inch in length. They belong to the same family of frogs that includes the poison arrow or poison dart frogs. And as with those species of arboreal, or tree-living, frogs, this guy is poisonous. Scientists discovered something interesting about these frogs. Many of them acquire their poison from the food they eat. They know this because in captivity, poison arrow frogs become less toxic. What scientists believe is that out in the wild, they're eating things like tiny poisonous spiders, and they're actually extracting the spiders' poison. Then they use that poison in their skin to protect themselves.

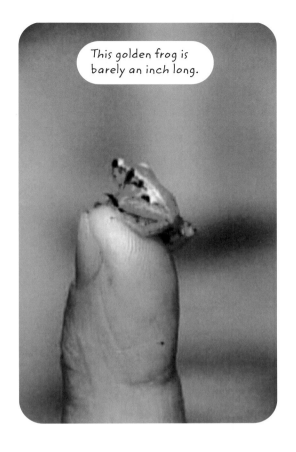

This golden frog is barely an inch long.

These animals can spend their entire lives in these bromeliads. Tank bromeliads will collect lots of water. The frogs will live and swim in them. They will eat there and breed there. You're probably wondering, "What are those little tadpoles going to eat there when they hatch?" The female will lay unfertilized eggs, little ova. And those ova will be eaten by hertadpoles. This is all happening in this little microcosmos, the little microworld we call a tank bromeliad.

Can someone get this frog off my face?

He's just hopped from my hand to the tip of my finger, and I think he's eyeing my head. Don't do it, buddy! I'm going to slip him right back to his home. He'll hop right down. Doink! Doink! Cool stuff! Well, it's time to get back to Iwokrama. I'm going to trade in this expensive airplane for a cheap pair of walking shoes and find some more of those giants of Guyana.

Almost untouched, Guyana's rain forest is one of the best-kept secrets in South America. In fact, part of the reason some of Guyana's animals are so big is because they haven't fallen prey to hunters or to the loss of habitat.

Oh, look at this. This is what's left of a termite mound. It's been totally excavated. Whatever dug this was huge. And there's something in here. Aha! It's a toad. Look at the size of this creature! It's a toad covered with termites, but a toad nonetheless. This is *bufo marinus*. What is really cool about these animals is that they are the largest toads in the world. You can find *bufo marinus* living throughout Central and South America, but here in Guyana you get giant ones. If you saw the normal *bufo marinus* toad, you'd say, "Man that's a big toad." But this creature weighs two pounds.

What's in this termite mound?

Yuck! This toad is covered with termites.

From the tip of its muscle to the tip of its cloaca, or vent, this creature is probably 8 or 9 inches in length. The total length from the toes to the nose is about 14 inches. It is a huge toad!

This creature can swallow a mouse opossum, or even a bird, in just two gulps. It will grab on and sort of gag and then take its little hands and feed it into its mouth. I would never feed myself with this toad, because even though it can't scratch or bite me, it is deadly. It has parotid glands, and they manufacture a poison called bufotoxin. If you ate this guy, you could die. If you survived, you'd have learned your lesson and you'd leave this species alone. The first defense is camouflage, and the second defense is the poison. This species is found throughout the tropics, but you only find them this big here in Guyana. I'm going to release this creature, and we'll continue our search.

Meet Mr. Bufo marinus.

He can shove a whole bird into his mouth.

Well, so far we've seen a giant turtle, a giant waterfall, a giant frog, and some giant potholes. Now let's see what other cool surprises Guyana has to offer. Here's a big pile of rocks with a clump of lush vegetation around it. This is an ideal habitat for lizards, scorpions, and snakes.

Look at this! Its tail makes it a very interesting serpent. And it's a tail with a pile of skin on the end, which means a rattlesnake. This is a very venomous snake, so I'm going to move very, very cautiously. Look at this beautiful, beautiful snake. This is a neotropical rattlesnake. There are some interesting differences between this rattlesnake and its North American counterparts. From the head to one third of its body it has stripes. Then it has diamonds that end at a tiny rattle. That's what makes these animals so special to me—the two unique patterns on one body.

This neotropical rattlesnake is very beautiful ... and very venomous.

As are all rattlers, it is venomous. And the venom on this species, the *durisis,* is pretty potent. It is designed to immobilize its prey and break down the tissue. If you respect this rattler, it will respect you. So I'm going to place this creature back into the rocks and see what else there is to be discovered here in beautiful Guyana.

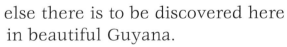

The Rupununi River is home to another of Guyana's giants. Not only are the animals huge, but the plants are as well. You find the largest lily pads in the world in Guyana. I've traveled all

Guyana has the largest lily pads in the world. They're huge!

the way up the Rupununi River to this little place called Karanambu. And that's the person I'm looking for. This is Diane McTurk. She's proprietor of Karanambu, this little ranch where you can come stay and appreciate the rain forest. She's also the keeper of some very special creatures that happen to be some of the largest and rarest mammals you'll find in South America.

Right now, Diane is trying to draw out these animals by calling them by the pet names she's given them. And here comes somebody. It's an otter. Diane knows these

The Rupununi River leads us to Karanambu.

Come up here, river otters!

24

There's one!

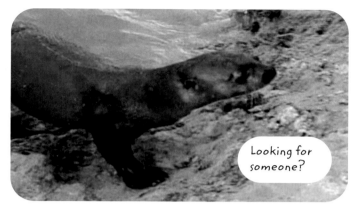

Looking for someone?

animals and works with them on a regular basis. But keep in mind that these are wild animals with a powerful bite. So they need lots of respect and lots of space. I'm very excited about this because we've got giant river otters here, and Diane is feeding them

Careful, Diane. He's got a powerful bite.

fish. The giant river otter of South America is the largest of the world's otters. It reaches lengths of 6 feet and weights of 70 pounds or more.

What's interesting about
this particular pod, or group, is
that two of them are individuals
that she raised. They were
orphaned and came into her
care. She mastered the art of
raising otters and then figured
out how to get them back into
the wild and keep them there.
And now, true wild otters have
come in and joined this pod.
These are considered the most
endangered mammals in the
neotropics. They are critically
close to extinction.
It looks like the
sun is setting,
which means we
are losing light.
I think we better
head back.
Thank you,
Diane!

That was
amazing,
Diane!

The giant river otter is the most endangered mammal in the neotropics.

Finally...its nighttime.

Time to find some nocturnal animals.

My goal is to get deeper into the jungle, and to do that we'll follow the Rupununi River. This is my favorite time to explore a rain forest, because at night everything wakes up. Eighty percent of the wildlife living here is nocturnal, which means they are active at night.

And 80 percent live above the forest floor. So we'll just keep our eyes up.

Look at that, look at that right there. This creature is my little friend. I'm trying to get him so he doesn't get away. Come here, sweetheart. He almost gave me a nice little nip. His tail is very strong, and so is his bite.

That's why I'm holding him by his tail. Now don't worry, I'm not hurting this animal. I want to be able to show you what makes this guy so cool. It's a mouse opossum. Isn't it neat? It's one of the smallest opossums you can find living in the Americas. It belongs to the same family that most opossums belong to, *didelphidae,* but these are very interesting, ancient-looking creatures. Look at the way his

I'd better hold him by the tail.

prehensile tail is wrapping around my finger. It's functioning as a fifth limb to secure itself as it moves through its rain forest habitat. This is an exciting discovery, because normally if you want to find these creatures, you have to go to the canopy. This one ventured closer to the forest floor in search of food. They're insect, fruit, and nectar eaters. Look at how quickly he moves in the nighttime habitat.

Now what's interesting about these opossums is that many of them, nearly half in the New World tropics, don't have a pouch. And he's a jumper, too. There goes our opossum! He went back to the canopy. What's great about this habitat is that there are lots of species to be found here. So let's take a look.

I hope you're ready for an adventure because I've got something exciting in store for us. What we're going to do is follow this little tributary. All sorts of creatures from caiman to matamata turtles make their way and survive in this tiny little waterway. So let's just check it out.

Oh, this reminds me to bring up another thing I should tell you about around here: safety. You can step on an electric ray or a poisonous ray. You can get zapped by an electric eel. Or you could end up on the menu for a large caiman. And there are some seriously large caiman in this habitat. Look at that! I nearly stepped on a speckled caiman. This is a good example of why you have to be so careful everywhere you walk. All right, caiman, you go your way and I'll go mine.

This kingfisher doesn't look too happy.

Look at the kingfisher just sleeping up there. It's a beautiful giant Amazon kingfisher. He's looking at me as if to say, "Hey, turn off the lights!" Let's keep looking.

I knew I saw something else. This serpent was lurking about in the branches. It's a great discovery, this great constrictor, perhaps not great in size but great in its ability to carve out a nice existence here above the water, looming out in the trees searching for prey. It is *corallus,* a tree boa. When I first captured him, he actually got me on my thumb and finger. These tree boas have very, very long teeth. They're not fangs, since they're not producing venom.

I think I see something up there.

Wow! A tree boa.

One of their favorite things to eat, in addition to the occasional tree frog or lizard, is birds. And when you're going after birds, you need to have teeth that are long enough to get through the feathers into the flesh to really secure the prey.

Now I'm just holding him very gently in my hands. I don't want him to struggle too much. And I've secured his head. See this coil he's exhibiting? This coil is the second technique for securing and finally killing the prey. It's called constriction, a deadly hug. And as you

He's squeezing my arm in a deadly hug.

See the divots along its lip?

can see, this little snake can actually pop up a couple of veins on my arm.

Something else that's kind of neat about this critter are those divots along the lower part of the lip. They're designed to detect something that is emitted from prey. They're close to the nairs, to the nostrils, so you would think they're part of the olfactory, or smelling, system. Wrong. They sense heat. This creature can not only sniff out and taste its way to prey with that highly sensitive tongue, but it can also detect the warmth that radiates from warm-blooded animals.

They sense heat while its nose sniffs out prey.

The tree boa has three ways to find its prey—smell, taste, and even body heat.

In the case of these branches, perhaps it's a bird such as a sleeping rufus kingfisher, or a little kiskadee, or a little flycatcher. Whatever it is, if it's warm and it's sleeping at night, it's in trouble because it is potential prey for this tree boa, which hunts at night.

Now if you like this reptile, wait until you see what I have in store for you next. Because what we're going to do is release this beautiful constricting tree boa back into the branches, and meander down this creek, which is brimming with very large reptiles. We're going to veer off to a smaller little creek and hopefully, I'm going to show you another reptile—not a snake, and certainly a lot larger than this tree boa.

There. He's back up in the branches.

This creek is full of reptiles.

Here's one of this ecosystem's greatest treasures.

See that? This is a hidden treasure of this ecosystem: little baby black caimans. These hatchlings are less than a year old, and they're protected by a little satellite that moves about. And that satellite is big mama. Let's check these babies out.

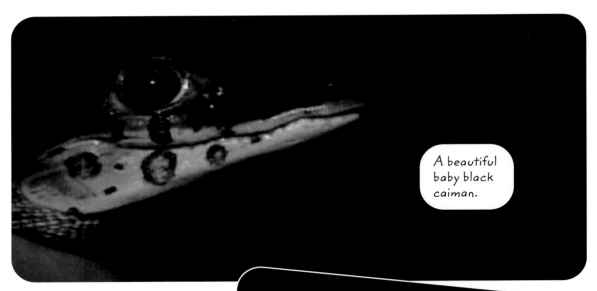

A beautiful baby black caiman.

This one right there probably came out last year. In the wild, food for these animals consists of fish and turtles. They are the largest caimans in the world and can grow up to 17 feet in length. At that size, they're eating mammals such as deer.

Mama caiman swims around constantly, watching over her babies.

I'd better let this one go now.

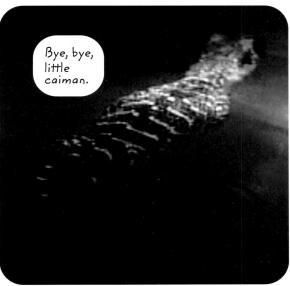

Bye, bye, little caiman.

Oh, there's mom. It's time for me to let this little black caiman venture off and time for me to move on myself.

If you look around me now, you see I'm in a very different place. This habitat is extreme. It's dry and flat and grassy. This is a savanna. I sent word to some of the local people to keep their eyes out for a really interesting creature.

Here's a very different place...a savanna.

We have to walk really quiet.

Shh....Look under that tree.

Rumor has it that these ranchers have spotted it. So where's the anteater? Right over by that tree. Okay, we want to walk really quiet. It's sleeping against the tree, and it's actually snoring. I didn't know an anteater could snore, but this guy is snoring.

An anteater taking a nap.

I want to try to wake it up, but not startle it. So I want us all to freeze, so that when he wakes up he won't see us. His vision is not very good, but he'll be listening. I'm just going to rattle the grass to see if I can get him up.

Look at that. He can really move!

His head's like a funnel.

Watch it, he's moving. We're just going to slowly follow him. Now he's actually galloping!

Look at this creature's head—it's like a funnel. Inside its mouth is a sticky, 24-inch-long tongue. It flickers in and out of that mouth 150 times in a minute as it raids that termite mound. This gives him the ability to eat 30,000 termites in a single day! Boy, we could have used this guy when we were rebuilding our house when we discovered our little termite problem.

He belongs to a group called the xenarthrans. This group includes sloths, armadillos, and anteaters. And this guy, *myrmecophaga tridactyla*, is the largest of the anteaters. They can reach a length of nearly 5 feet and a weight of 90 pounds.

This creature can eat 30,000 termites in just one day!

I'll see you next time for another great adventure.

This guy took us for a little jaunt in the savanna, but he brought us back to where he was sleeping. I think this beautiful *myrmecophaga tridactyla,* one of the many giants of Guyana, is going to go take a nap, and I've got to go find my vehicle. See you, Mr. Anteater.

Well, our exciting adventure in Guyana has come to an end. I'll see you on our next great adventure on the Jeff Corwin Experience.

Glossary

amphibian a class of cold-blooded organisms including frogs and toads

arboreal animals that spend most of their time in trees

bufotoxin a moderately potent poison secreted in the skin of toads

caiman a South American crocodilian, similar to an alligator

camouflage coloring that helps an animal blend in with its environment

canopy the upper level of the rain forest

dulap the flap of skin under the chin of an anole lizard

epiphytic plants that take nutrients from air and rain

extinction when no members of a species exist

habitat a place where animals and plants live naturally together

mammals warm-blooded animals that give birth to live babies and feed them with milk

ova egg

parotid glands large salivary glands below and in front of the ears

predator an animal that kills and eats other animals

prey the animal hunted by a predator

pristine clean and unspoiled

rain forests tropical forests that get a lot of rain

rendered melted down

reptile a cold-blooded, usually egg-laying animal such as a snake or lizard

savanna a tropical or subtropical grassland

serpents snakes

venom a poison used by snakes to attack their prey or defend themselves

venomous having a gland that produces poison for self-defense or hunting

Index